CONTENTS

Freedom Programme for Men Workbook

Section 1

1.1. Introduction

Welcome to the Freedom Programme for men.
Since 2002 I have provided the Freedom Programme for men in the form of a weekend course. I have always insisted that any man who is still in a relationship is accompanied by his female partner. I am now approaching retirement and may not be able to provide any more weekends although I have received hundreds of requests for them. So in response I have created this course.

'Misogyny' is an ancient Greek word meaning hatred of women. Abusers hate women. That is why they use violent and controlling behaviour. This principle also applies to same sex abuse because these abusers see their victims as women. Anyone who doubts that this form of violence and abuse is motivated by hatred should consider the case of the man who blinded Tina Nash. Only a deep and powerful loathing could have motivated him.

Men who have completed my two day weekend courses have thanked me for helping them to see themselves in a mirror. If you approach this workbook Home Study Course with an open mind and a genuine desire to change you too could benefit in this way. How hard can it be to treat the person you are supposed to love with respect and affection?

The workbook must be used in conjunction with the book 'Living With The Dominator'. Please read it before starting the workbook. Then work steadily through the programme following the instructions on how to refer to the book. It is useful to read each chapter again before starting the appropriate section. 'Living With The Dominator' can be bought from Amazon, and from my website, **www.freedomprogramme.co.uk**

1.2. Statistics quiz. How much do I remember from the book?

Tick the boxes. The answers follow so you can check your score.

The Quiz

1. Domestic violence accounts for

    2% ☐   10% ☐   25% ☐

    of all reported violent crime.

2. In Britain, a woman is killed by a violent partner or former partner every:

    3 days ☐   every week ☐   every 2 weeks ☐

3. It is estimated that

    3% ☐   13% ☐   33% ☐

    of women experience domestic violence in their lifetime.

4. How many times on average is a woman assaulted before she seeks help?

    5 ☐   15 ☐   35 ☐

5. On average, how many men a year are killed by their female partners or former partners?

    22 ☐   52 ☐   112 ☐

freedomprogramme@btinternet.com
www.freedomprogramme.co.uk

6. On average, how many women a year are killed by their male partners or former partners?

12 ☐   52 ☐   112 ☐

7. How many women's refuges are there in England?

275 ☐   1000 ☐   5000 ☐

8. Is a woman:

less likely ☐   just as likely ☐   more likely ☐

to be assaulted when she is pregnant?

9. Domestic violence happens because of

drink ☐   drugs ☐   stress ☐

mental illness ☐   unemployment ☐

power / control ☐

10. What percentage of murder victims are men who have been killed by a partner or former partner?

4% ☐   40% ☐   80% ☐

11. In Britain, police receive a complaint about domestic violence every

60 seconds ☐   6 minutes ☐   6 hours ☐

12. In Britain, a woman is assaulted in her home every

6 seconds ☐   60 seconds ☐   6 minutes ☐

THE ANSWERS

1.   25% of all reported crime (Amnesty UK, 2006)

2.   Every 3 days (Home Office, 2007)

3.   33% (Home Office, 2007). My experience with the Freedom Programme leads me to believe it is higher. Many of us do not realise we are being abused.

4.   35 (Amnesty UK, 2006)

5.   22 (Home Office, 2007)

6.   112 (Home Office, 2007)

7.   275 (Women's Aid, 2004) and approximately 1500 animal refuges.

8.   Women are 3 times more likely to be injured when pregnant
(Refuge, 2007).

9.   Power / Control

10.   4% (Home Office, 2001)

11.   60 seconds (The Day to count, 2000, Elizabeth A. Stanko)

12.   6 seconds (The Day to count, 2000, Elizabeth A. Stanko)

Notes

Write your thoughts and feelings here to keep a record of your progress through the programme.

....

....

....

....

....

....

....

....

....

....

....

....

....

....

....

....

....

....

freedomprogramme@btinternet.com
www.freedomprogramme.co.uk

1.3. The Dominator and Mr Right

You will see from the statistics that most abusers are men and that they use abusive behaviour to keep us women under control. Now open your book at the picture of the Dominator on page 11. Read about each type of abuse. You can then add more examples of each type of abuse.

When you have done this, look at Mr Right on page 15. Read all the examples of non-abusive behaviour. We will return to study him in greater detail later in the course.

Question
Why do abusive men want to control women?

Answer... *The behaviour of the dominator is based upon his beliefs.*

Check your answer with page 13 of 'Living with the Dominator'

Sometimes we don't know what we believe. Sometimes we think we believe something when we actually believe something different.

Beliefs awareness exercise

Ask yourself, "Do I believe that is important to keep the air we breathe clean?"

Answer... *Yes I do*

Now ask yourself, "Do I drive a car?"

Answer... *Yes I do*

If the answer to both questions is yes, what do you actually believe? It is possible that you believe that your own comforts and needs are more important than the need to have clean air.

Ask yourself, "Do I disapprove of bullying?"

Answer... *Yes I do*

freedomprogramme@btinternet.com
www.freedomprogramme.co.uk

Now ask yourself, "Have I ever shouted at my children, partner or the dog?"

Answer...

If the answer to both questions is yes, what do you really believe about bullying?

Ask yourself, "Do I believe in keeping my body healthy?"

Answer...

Now ask yourself, "Do I smoke, drink or eat too much?"

Answer...

If the answer to both questions is yes, what do you really believe?

Ask yourself, "Do I believe women have a right to say no to sex?'

Answer...

Now ask yourself, "Have I ever nagged until she gives in?"

Answer...

Now ask yourself, "Have I huffed and puffed and sulked?"

Answer...

If the answer to two of the questions is yes, what do you really believe?

Congratulations! You have completed section 1. There is a lot to think about!

freedomprogramme@btinternet.com
www.freedomprogramme.co.uk

Notes

Write your thoughts and feelings here to keep a record of your progress through the programme.

....

....

....

....

....

....

....

....

....

....

....

....

....

....

....

....

....

....

....

freedomprogramme@btinternet.com
www.freedomprogramme.co.uk

Section 2. The Bully (Chapter 3, pages 17 – 25)

Each session begins with a quiz about the tactics of the Dominator. You may like to cover the answers with a piece of paper and then check them to see if you answered correctly.

Remember that the aim of the quiz is not so much to get all the all the answers right, but more to help you to identify and name abusive behaviour before you use it in future.

2.1. The Quiz

Tactics

1. Sulks
2. Tells his partner her tits are too small
3. Goes out of the room when her friends visit
4. Tells her it was only a push
5. Tells the kids that their mother is stupid
6. Expects his dinner to be ready whenever he walks through the door
7. Invites her friend to have a threesome
8. Tells her he will kill himself if she leaves

Answers

1. The Bully
2. The Headworker
3. The Jailer
4. The Liar
5. The Badfather
6. The King of the Castle
7. The Sexual Controller
8. The Persuader

2.2 Question Sheet for Session 2

After completing this work sheet you can check your answers on pages 17 – 25 of the book.

If you are serious about wanting to learn and change you need to think hard about all these questions and answer them in detail. If you skim through them you will be wasting your time. This course offers you a chance to think very clearly about the society in which you live and your reaction to it. You will need extra paper to properly answer all the questions in every section.

2.3. The tactics of the Bully

Make a list of as many as you can think of. Don't limit your answers to the specific questions I have posed. Add any other tactics that you can think of.

We are not asking for examples of violence. Concentrate on intimidation.

How does the Bully use his body language to intimidate his partner?

How does he use every bit of his body?

Think of his fingers, toes and eyes.

Don't ask what he says, but how he says it? Think of his tone of voice.

Answers

....

....

....

....

....

2.4. What does the Bully believe?

What does he believe about violence, "real" men and the status of women compared to men?

Does he believe women need controlling/protecting?

What does he believe about men who don't bully women?

Answers

....

....

....

....

....

2.5. Where do his beliefs come from and how are they reinforced?

What messages does he receive from watching sports and observing institutions such as the armed forces?

What messages does he receive from popular and traditional culture? - Only discuss your OWN culture.

Consider history, religion, music and all forms of media, including film.

What messages does he get from the law and the legal system?

Write down where you think his beliefs come from and how they are reinforced. Include specific examples of the messages he is getting from all these sources.

Answers

....

....

....

....

....

2.6. Which of these beliefs do YOU share?
Think carefully and answer as honestly as you can.
e.g What do you think about men who do not bully women?
Do you believe that shouting is not abusive?

Answers

....

....

....

....

....

2.7. How are women affected by being bullied in this way?
How do women feel all the time?
How may a woman behave? Really try to imagine yourself in this situation.

     freedomprogramme@btinternet.com
www.freedomprogramme.co.uk

Answers

....

....

....

....

....

2.8. How does the Friend behave and what does he believe?
Look at his body language.
What are his eyes like? What is his voice like?
What does he believe about women?
Does he like the company women?
What does he believe about the use of violence?
How hard can it be to behave like this consistently?

Answers

....

....

....

....

....

Congratulations! You have now completed section 2.

Notes

Write your thoughts and feelings here to keep a record of your progress through the programme.

....

....

....

....

....

....

....

....

....

....

....

....

....

....

....

....

....

....

....

....

Section 3. The Badfather (Chapter 4, pages 27 – 34)

Remember that the aim of the quiz is not so much to get all the all the answers right, but more to help you to identify and name abusive behaviour before you use it in future.

3.1. The Quiz

Tactics

1. Smashes his partners possessions
2. Tells other people her secrets
3. Says her friend made a pass at him
4. Says she started it
5. Uses the courts to get access.
6. Nags until she agrees to sex
7. Takes all the money
8. Says, 'Please have me back. I have nowhere else to go!'

Answers

1. The Bully
2. The Headworker
3. The Jailer
4. The Liar
5. The Badfather
6. The Sexual Controller
7. The King of the Castle
8. The Persuader

How was your score?

3.2 Question sheet for Section 3

After completing this work sheet you can check your answers on pages 27 – 34 of the book. Please note that the Badfather is not always the biological father of the children he is using to abuse their mother.

3.3. Tactics of the Badfather

Make a list of as many as you can think of. Don't limit your answers to the specific questions I have posed. Add any other tactics that you can think of.

How does the Badfather ensure that his partner cannot control the children?
How does he use the children to isolate her?
How does he use the children to persuade her to have him back after violence?
How does he use the children to intimidate her? Note, he can do this when they are still together or when they have separated.

Answers

....

....

....

....

....

3.4. His beliefs

What does he believe about childcare and real men?

Does he believe that women can manage children without a man, any man, in the house?

Who does he think has rights? Women, children, or him?

Does he believe violence affects children? Does he care?

What does he think about fathers who change nappies?

Answers

....

....

....

....

....

3.5. Origins and reinforcements

Write down where you think his beliefs come from and how they are reinforced. Include specific examples of how these institutions reinforce his beliefs

Consider political propaganda

Consider the messages he gets from the media about the need for a father figure?

What do the family courts tell him?

What message does he get from pressure groups?

What messages he had from other agencies?

What messages does he get from other men?

 freedomprogramme@btinternet.com
www.freedomprogramme.co.uk

Answers

....

....

....

....

....

3.6. Which beliefs do YOU share?

e.g. Do you believe the children are not affected by your violence?
Do you believe women can bring up the children without a man?
Do you believe it is possible to be a good father when you are
abusing the mother of the children? Would you change nappies?

Answers

....

....

....

....

....

freedomprogramme@btinternet.com
www.freedomprogramme.co.uk

3.7. How are women affected?

How is a woman affected when he uses access and the courts to harass her?

How is she affected when he uses the children to isolate her?

How is she affected when he turns the children against her?

Think very carefully about how you would you feel if you were in her situation.

Answers

....

....

....

....

....

3.8. The Goodfather

How does the Goodfather behave to their mother in front of the children?

How does he behave towards the children?

What does he believe about childcare?

Does he change nappies?

What sort of role model is he?

Is he an asset to a family?

Answers

....

....

....

....

Congratulations! You have completed Section 3.

www.freedomprogramme.co.uk

Notes

Write your thoughts and feelings here to keep a record of your progress through the programme.

....

....

....

....

....

....

....

....

....

....

....

....

....

....

....

....

....

....

....

freedomprogramme@btinternet.com
www.freedomprogramme.co.uk

Section 4. The Effects of Domestic Abuse on Children (Chapter 5, pages 35 - 46)

Remember that the aim of the quiz is not so much to get all the all the answers right, but more to help you to identify and name abusive behaviour before you use it in future.

4.1. The Quiz

Tactics

1. Sulks
2. Tells his partner she is ugly
3. Causes a row when she wants to go out
4. Denies he was abusive when challenged
5. Refuses to 'baby-sit'
6. Burns the breakfast deliberately
7. Threatens to report her to social services if she leaves him
8. Rapes her when she is asleep

Answers

1. The Bully
2. The Headworker
3. The Jailer
4. The Liar
5. The Badfather
6. The King of the Castle
7. The Persuader
8. The Sexual Controller

4.2. Question sheet for Section 4

After completing this work sheet you can check your answers on pages 35 – 46 of the book. This is a crucially important section of the course. The abuse that children experience when they are young can ruin their lives.

4.3. What do children need?

We divide children in to 3 groups

The first group to consider is, the pregnant mother, an unborn child and a newborn baby. What do they need? You may like to consider the needs of the mother first and then see that the other needs flow from them. Make a list of as many needs as you can think of. Keep your answers simple and do not use jargon.

Many men have told me that before doing this session they had never thought about what children need.

Answers

....

....

....

....

....

The next category deals with the needs of a six-year-old. Please list everything that you can think of that a six-year-old needs to develop successfully. Be specific. Don't just say things like "care." Define precisely what this means.

Answers

....

....

....

....

....

What does a teenager need? Consider whether the needs of the
first two categories are linked to the needs of the teenager. They
also have individual needs which may differ from the first two
categories.

Answers

....

....

....

....

....

 freedomprogramme@btinternet.com
www.freedomprogramme.co.uk

4.4. Effects of domestic abuse on children

How is the first group affected by being exposed to the tactics of the Dominator?

Consider how the mother is affected, then discuss how the way she is affected impacts on the unborn child and the new baby.

Answers

....

....

....

....

....

Now consider the six-year-old. Consider that our child is now six years older. Remember all the effects on the first group. Now consider the situation six years later. See how much worse things are. Consider the beliefs our six-year-old will be developing. You should need extra paper if you are answering these questions thoroughly.

Answers

....

....

....

....

....

Finally, have a look at the teenager. All the effects on the baby and the six-year-old have now accumulated. How are teenagers affected and what will they now believe?

Answers

....

....

....

....

....

4.5. Home improvements

Now list how the lives of a pregnant women, unborn child and newborn child are improved without the Dominator. This is a very important part of the course.

Imagine he has left or stopped being abusive when the mother is six months pregnant. She will then have the last three months without abuse. How will everything have improved for her and her baby?

Be specific. List the things she can now do for herself and for the baby.

Could YOU improve your family situation by changing your behaviour or simply leaving them in peace?

Answers

....

....

....

....

....

freedomprogramme@btinternet.com
www.freedomprogramme.co.uk

Now list the improvements for a six-year-old. The Dominator has left, or changed, when the child is five. The mother and child have been free of abuse for a year.

Answers

....

....

....

....

....

Now list the improvements for a fifteen-year-old. The Dominator has left or changed when our child is thirteen. Mother and teenager have been free of abuse for two years.

Answers

....

....

....

....

....

Congratulations! You have now completed section 4.

Notes

Write your thoughts and feelings here to keep a record of your progress through the programme.

....

....

....

....

....

....

....

....

....

....

....

....

....

....

....

....

....

....

....

freedomprogramme@btinternet.com
www.freedomprogramme.co.uk

Section 5. The Headworker (Chapter 6, pages 47 - 56)

5.1. The Quiz

1. Grits his teeth
2. Has affairs with other women
3. Has affairs with his partners friends
4. Tells her she made him abusive
5. Denies paternity ("They are not my fucking kids!")
6. Comes and goes as he pleases. Treats the home like a hotel
7. Cries on the doorstep
8. Ejaculates prematurely and blames her

Answers

1. The Bully
2. The Headworker
3. The Jailer
4. The Liar
5. The Badfather
6. The King of the Castle
7. The Persuader
8. The Sexual Controller

5.2 Question sheet for Section 5

After completing this work sheet you can check your answers on pages 47 – 56 of the book.

5.3. Tactics of the Headworker

How does the Headworker make his partner feel ugly, useless, stupid and mad? Make a list of as many ways as you can think of. Don't limit your answers to the specific questions I have posed. Add any other tactics that you can think of.

Answers

....

....

....

....

....

5.4. What does the Headworker believe?

What does he believe about the competence and intelligence of all women?
What does he believe women are placed on this earth for?
What is their function?

Answers

....

....

....

....

5.5. Where do such beliefs come from and how are they reinforced?

Consider language. What words are generally used about women to indicate that they are stupid?

What words indicate that they are pieces of meat?

Think of the history of psychiatry.

Think of magazines. Think of music and insidious messages in advertising. Think of a very famous radio presenter who continuously makes sexist jokes. Think about the content of jokes about women.

Answers

....

....

....

....

....

5.6.Which of these beliefs do YOU share?

Do you believe women are equal to men?

What words do you use about women?

What jokes have you told or laughed at?

Answers

....

....

....

....

....

freedomprogramme@btinternet.com
www.freedomprogramme.co.uk

5.7. Effects of those beliefs on behaviour

How is a woman affected by living with a Headworker?

How is she affected by all his tactics?

How are all women affected by living in a society which holds the beliefs of the Headworker?

Think very carefully about how YOU would you feel if you were in her situation.

Answers

....

....

....

....

....

5.8. The Confidence Booster

How does the Confidence Booster behave towards his partner?

Does he like her?

What does he believe about women?

How hard can it be to treat the woman you are supposed to love with affection and respect?

Answers

....

....

....

....

....

Congratulations again!

        freedomprogramme@btinternet.com
www.freedomprogramme.co.uk

Notes

Write your thoughts and feelings here to keep a record of your progress through the programme.

....

....

....

....

....

....

....

....

....

....

....

....

....

....

....

....

....

....

....

....

freedomprogramme@btinternet.com
www.freedomprogramme.co.uk

Section 6. The Jailer (Chapter 7, pages 57 - 63)

6.1. The Quiz

Tactics

1. Displays weapons
2. Makes his partner feel guilty
3. Says that her friends don't really like her
4. Says he was abusive because he was drunk
5. Says she can leave but the children must stay
6. Says he "helps her" with the housework
7. Threatens to kill the children if she leaves
8. Bribes her to have sex by offering to buy a new winter coat

Answers

1. The Bully
2. The Headworker
3. The Jailer
4. The Liar
5. The Badfather
6. The King of the Castle
7. The Persuader
8. The Sexual Controller

6.2 Question sheet for Section 6

After completing this work sheet you can check your answers on pages 57 – 63 of the book.

6.3. Tactics used by the Jailer

Make a list of as many as you can think of. Don't limit your answers to the specific questions I have posed. Add any other tactics that you can think of.

How does the Jailor stop his partner seeing her friends?

How does he stop her working?

How does he keep her in the house?

How does he cut her off from her family?

Answers

....

....

....

....

....

freedomprogramme@btinternet.com
www.freedomprogramme.co.uk

6.4. The Jailer's beliefs

Where does the Jailor believe women should be?

What would he believe about a man who did not keep his partner locked away?

What does he believe all women will all do if they get out of the house?

What does he believe all women are?

Answers

....

....

....

....

....

6.5. Where do all these beliefs come from and how are they reinforced?

Consider language and commonly used phrases.

Consider social traditions, sports and education.

What do you know about the history of women and universities in Britain?

Think about social policies. How were women in Britain treated after World War Two? Think about advertisements.

When did women get the vote?

Answers

....

....

....

....

....

6.6. Which beliefs do YOU share?

e.g. Do you believe you have the right to prevent your partner from working or going out with her friends?

What do you think she would do if she went out without you?

How do you think women who are successful in business achieved this success?

Answers

....

....

....

....

....

6.7. How are women affected by the Jailer.

When you answer this question imagine how YOU would react if this was happening to you.

How is a woman affected by being kept in the house?

How is she affected by being prevented from working?

How is she affected by being cut off from her friends and family?

How would YOU like to live like a prisoner?

Answers

....

....

....

....

....

6.8. The Liberator

How does the Liberator behave? Consider his reactions to his partner's desire to work or get out of the house and meet her friends?

How does he behave to her friends and family?

What does he believe about women?

Does he trust his partner?

Is he a pleasant companion?

How hard can it be to trust the woman you are supposed to love?

Answers

....

....

....

....

....

Congratulations again!

freedomprogramme@btinternet.com
www.freedomprogramme.co.uk

Notes

Write your thoughts and feelings here to keep a record of your progress through the programme.

....

....

....

....

....

....

....

....

....

....

....

....

....

....

....

....

....

....

....

....

Section 7. The Sexual Controller (Chapter 8, pages 65 - 76)

7.1. The Quiz

Tactics

1. Stalks his partner or ex partner
2. Makes her think she is going mad by moving furniture and then denying it
3. Goes everywhere with her
4. Says he was abusive because he was jealous
5. Asks the children to check up on her
6. Says she must be a lesbian if she says no to sex
   (Bless him! He thinks it is an insult!)
7. Ignores the housework until she does it
8. Says that he will see a Relate counsellor if she takes him back

Answers

1. The Bully
2. The Headworker
3. The Jailer
4. The Liar
5. The Badfather
6. The Sexual Controller
7. The King of the Castle
8. The Persuader

freedomprogramme@btinternet.com
www.freedomprogramme.co.uk

7.2 Question sheet for Section 7.

After completing this work sheet you can check your answers on pages 65 – 76 of the book.

7.3. What tactics does the Sexual Controller use?

Make a list of as many as you can think of. Don't limit your answers to the specific questions I have posed. Add any other tactics that you can think of.

How does he make his partner have sex when she does not want it?

Answers

....

....

....

....

....

How does he use sex as a weapon to degrade and defeat her?

Answers

....

....

....

....

....

 freedomprogramme@btinternet.com
www.freedomprogramme.co.uk

7.4. What does he believe about men and women?

What does he believe women are actually for?

Does he believe they have any other function apart from providing sex?

What does he believe about their rights and his rights?

Does he like the company of women?

Answers

....

....

....

....

....

7.5. Where do these beliefs come from and how are they reinforced?

Law. Media. Magazines. Newspapers. The medical profession. Fine art. Religion. Music. History. Give examples. Think very carefully about the society in which we all live.

Answers

....

....

....

....

....

7.6. Which of these beliefs do YOU share?

e.g Do you believe your partner has any right to say no to sex?

Do you believe that 'no' means 'yes'?

What sort of newspapers or magazines do YOU read?

What kind of jokes do you tell or laugh at?

Answers

....

....

....

....

....

7.7. Effects of the Sexual Controller on women

How is a woman affected by living with a sexual controller? Try to imagine how you would react to such relentless abuse.

How are all women affected by living in a society that holds these beliefs?

Answers

....

....

....

....

....

7.8. The Lover

How does he behave sexually?

Does he show affection to his partner?

How difficult can it be to treat the woman you are supposed to love with affection and respect?

What does he believe about women?

Does he like women?

Does he like their company?

Would he go to a lap-dancing club?

If not, why not?

What does he believe about sex?

Answers

....

....

....

....

....

Women find this session to be painful but they are reassured when they realise that this is not personal. The Sexual Controller hates ALL women, not only them.

Notes

Write your thoughts and feelings here to keep a record of your progress through the programme.

....

....

....

....

....

....

....

....

....

....

....

....

....

....

....

....

....

....

....

....

www.freedomprogramme.co.uk

Section 8. The King of the Castle (Chapter 9, pages 77 - 86)

8.1. The Quiz

Tactics

1. Kicks walls
2. Does not call his partner by her name
3. Goes out without taking the key
4. Says he hit her because he suffers from "Gulf War Syndrome"
5. Contradicts her instructions to the children
6. Pretends he can't cook
7. Says, 'Have me back or I will follow you to the ends of the earth'
8. Tells her she is unnatural if she refuses sex

Answers

1. The Bully
2. The Headworker
3. The Jailer
4. The Liar
5. The Badfather
6. The King of the Castle
7. The Persuader
8. The Sexual Controller

freedomprogramme@btinternet.com
www.freedomprogramme.co.uk

8.2 Question sheet for Section 8.

After completing this work sheet you can check your answers on pages 77 – 86 of the book.

8.3. Tactics of the King of the Castle.

Make a list of as many as you can think of. Don't limit your answers to the specific questions I have posed. Add any other tactics that you can think of.

The King of the Castle is subtle. He may not stomp in to his partner's life and start ordering her around. How does he manipulate her so she will do all household tasks without being aware of it?
How does he get her to do all the washing? How does he get her to do the cooking? How does he get her to do the cleaning? How does he make sure she knows where things are and that she puts things away? What is the question he will ask?
How does he get her to be in charge of menus? What question will he ask? How does he begin to control the money? How will he ensure he is in charge of the television?

Answers

....

....

....

....

....

freedomprogramme@btinternet.com
www.freedomprogramme.co.uk

8.4. The beliefs of the King of the Castle
What does he believe about the status of housework?
What sort of people should therefore do his housework?
Would a "real man" pay someone to do his housework?
What does he believe about men who do their share of housework?"

Answers

....

....

....

....

....

8.5. Where do these beliefs come from and how are they reinforced?
Consider his childhood. Look at advertisements. Consider soap opera, films and books. What are women seen to be doing? Consider social policies and commonly used phrases that describe women?

Answers

....

....

....

....

....

8.6. Which beliefs do YOU share?

Do you expect your partner to act as an unpaid servant?

How much respect can you feel for someone you treat like that?

Answers

....

....

....

....

....

8.7. How is a woman affected by the tactics used by the King of the Castle?

How is she affected by being treated as a skivvy without rights or respect?

How are all women affected by the beliefs of the society in which we live?

Think very carefully about how YOU would you feel if you were in her situation. How would you react if someone treated you like this?

Answers

....

....

....

....

....

8.8. How does the Partner behave?

He is the non abusive counterpart to the King of the Castle. What does he do around the house and what does he believe? How hard can it be to treat the woman you are supposed to love as an equal?

Answers

....

....

....

....

....

Congratulations! You are getting close to completing the whole programme.

Notes

Write your thoughts and feelings here to keep a record of your progress through the programme.

....

....

....

....

....

....

....

....

....

....

....

....

....

....

....

....

....

....

....

....

Section 9. The Liar (Chapter 10, pages 87 – 97)

9.1. The Quiz

Tactics.

1. Swings his foot
2. Hides his partner's shoes
3. Tells her she must be suffering from PMT
4. Says she must have him back because he has cancer
5. Says any red-blooded man would kill his wife if he found her in bed with another man
6. Hits her when the children are in the house
7. Has his own chair that no one else is allowed to use
8. Asks the surgeon to stitch her up tight after Childbirth

Answers

1. The Bully
2. The Jailer
3. The Headworker
4. The Persuader
5. The Liar
6. The Badfather
7. The King of Castle
8. The Sexual Controller

9.2 Question sheet for Section 9

Before completing this work sheet you may find it helpful to visit my website **www.freedomprogramme.co.uk.** Click on THE DVD section and watch the DVD clip which explains this section. Then open the book at page 88 and look at 'Rules of the Game'.

After completing this work sheet you can check your answers on pages 77 – 86 of the book.

9.3. What are the rules?
Make a list of eight "Rules of the Game."

Use phrases like;

- "Women should…"
- "She should always…"
- "She should never…"
- "I should be able to…"

Write these rules in the voice of the Dominator.

Answers

....

....

....

....

....

....

9.4. Abusive Tactics

Have a look at the Dominator on page 11 and note an example of which aspect of the Dominator keeps which rule in place. For example, "She should never answer back" would be kept in place by the Bully.

Answers You can note them at the side of your rules above. Initials such as KOC (King of the Castle) will suffice.

9.5. Breaking the rules

How does a woman break the rules? - She often does not know what the rules are.

However one of the rules is that she should <u>always</u> know what the rules are.

When considering how she breaks the rules, look at the **list of rules** you have written.

A woman could break each rule in many different ways, either accidentally or deliberately.

(Write these examples in her voice E.g. 'I left him').

Answers

....

....

....

....

....

9.6. Excuses for violence.

Write his excuses in his voice. Use emotive language and remember that he has not yet hit her. Do not spare the bad language. Remember what he is convincing himself he should do.

Answers

....

....

....

....

....

9.7. Trying to put the rules back in place by using the tactics of the Liar

Write your answers in the voice of the Liar.

How does he now get the rules back in place using minimisation denial and blame?

Give examples of the "only" word to make the abuse seem less than it was.

What will he say to deny that anything happened?

What will he blame? Make a list including as many medical conditions as possible. Don't forget that he will rarely give the real reason, which is that his partner broke the rules. He will, however, blame her. How will he do that?

freedomprogramme@btinternet.com
www.freedomprogramme.co.uk

Answers

....

....

....

....

....

9.8. Which part of the cycle of "Rules of the Game" does he have to change to change his behaviour.

Answer

....

9.9. Is he is actually angry or is all this manufactured outrage?

Answer

....

9.10. How does the Liar's behaviour affect his victims?
How is a woman affected by all these complicated tactics?

Write the answers in her voice.

Answers

....

....

....

....

....

9.11. The Truthteller

An honest and accountable man. How does the opposite of the Liar
behave?

How hard can it be?

Answers

....

....

....

....

....

Well done!

That is the most complicated and most difficult part of the
programme to understand. It is also hard to accept that all this is
planned and you did not just 'lose your temper' or 'lash out'.

Notes

Write your thoughts and feelings here to keep a record of your progress through the programme.

....

....

....

....

....

....

....

....

....

....

....

....

....

....

....

....

....

....

....

....

freedomprogramme@btinternet.com
www.freedomprogramme.co.uk

Section 10. The Persuader (Chapter 11, pages 99 - 109)

10.1. The Quiz

Tactics

1. Drives too fast
2. Tells his partner that she is useless
3. Moves her to a strange town
4. Attempts suicide
5. Saying she made him abuse her
6. Says she is a bad mother
7. Refuses to have sex with her
8. Complains if she spends money on herself

Answers

1. The Bully
2. The Headworker
3. The Jailor
4. The Persuader
5. The Liar
6. The Badfather
7. The Sexual Controller
8. The King of the Castle

www.freedomprogramme.co.uk

10.2 Question sheet for Section 10

After completing this work sheet you can check your answers on pages 99 - 109 of the book.

10.3. Tactics of the Persuader

Make a list of as many as you can think of. Don't limit your answers to the specific questions I have posed. Add any other tactics that you can think of.

How does he make his partner feel sorry for him?
How does he indicate to her that he cannot cope without her?
Will he also use other people to influence her?
How will he use the children to persuade her to have him back?
What threats or promises may he make?
How will he use the excuses of the Liar to increase his level of control?

Answers

....
....
....
....
....

10.4. Beliefs of the Persuader

Who does he believe is responsible for his behaviour and his well-being?
Does he believe he has to pay any price for his violence and abuse?
Does he believe his behaviour is in any way unacceptable? Who is allowed to end the relationship? Who is not allowed to leave ?

Answers

....

....

....

....

....

10.5. Where do these beliefs come from and how are they reinforced?
Consider popular music, Country and Western and Blues.
Consider the law. Consider all the people he may go to for help. How might their responses reinforce his beliefs? E.g. He may visit a Bolloxologist for help to manage his 'anger'.

Answers

....

....

....

....

....

freedomprogramme@btinternet.com
www.freedomprogramme.co.uk

10.6. Which beliefs do YOU share?

e.g. Do you believe your partner is responsible for your well-being?

Do you believe women should look after men?

Do you take any responsibility for your actions?

Answers

....

....

....

....

....

10.7.How is a woman affected by the Persuader?

How is she affected by being made to feel sorry for him?

How is affected by his threats?

Think very carefully about how YOU would you feel and react if you were in her situation.

Answers

....

....

....

....

....

 freedomprogramme@btinternet.com
www.freedomprogramme.co.uk

10.8. The Negotiator

How does he behave if his partner wants to end the relationship?
Whose welfare will he consider? What does he believe? How hard
can it be to accept that someone has the right to leave you?

Answers

....

....

....

....

....

Only one more to go! I hope that was a little easier. 'What is a
Bolloxologist' you may ask? Or did you just guess?

Notes

Write your thoughts and feelings here to keep a record of your progress through the programme.

....

....

....

....

....

....

....

....

....

....

....

....

....

....

....

....

....

....

....

freedomprogramme@btinternet.com
www.freedomprogramme.co.uk

Section 11. Warning Signs (Chapter 12, pages 113 - 116)

11.1 The Quiz

Tactics

1. Cracks knuckles
2. Takes the buggy in the boot of the car
3. Uses the word "woman" as an insult
4. Promises to go to "anger management"   (Bolloxology)
5. Makes jokes about his partner to the children
6. Asks; "Where is my clean shirt?"
7. Visits a lap dancing club
8. Says he is abusive because he is insecure

Answers

1. The Bully
2. The Jailer
3. The Headworker
4. The Persuader
5. The Badfather
6. The King of the Castle
7. The Sexual Controller
8. The Liar

11.2 Question sheet for Section 11

Warning signs
Please write the answers to these questions from the point of view of a father advising his daughter how to avoid being involved with a dominator.

The Bully
Make a list of the warning signs for the Bully. What will she be able to see in the first two weeks of the relationship?

Answers

....

....

....

....

....

The Jailer
Make a list of the warning signs for the Jailer. What will she be able to see in the first two weeks of the relationship?

Answers

....

....

....

....

....

The Headworker

Make a list of the warning signs for the Headworker. What will she be able to see in the first two weeks of the relationship?

Answers

....

....

....

....

....

The Persuader

Make a list of the warning signs for the Persuader. What will she be able to see in the first two weeks of the relationship?

Answers

....

....

....

....

....

The Liar
Make a list of the warning signs for the Liar. What will she be able to see in the first two weeks of the relationship?

Answers

....

....

....

....

....

The Badfather
Make a list of the warning signs for the Badfather. What will she be able to see in the first two weeks of the relationship?

Answers

....

....

....

....

....

The King of the Castle
Make a list of the warning signs for the KOC. What will she be able to see in the first two weeks of the relationship?

Answers

....

....

....

....

....

The Sexual Controller

Make a list of the warning signs for the Sexual Controller. What will she be able to see in the first two weeks of the relationship?

Answers

....

....

....

....

....

freedomprogramme@btinternet.com
www.freedomprogramme.co.uk

11.3. Home improvements

Cover the next paragraph with a piece of paper until you have answered the question, then compare your answers with the ones that I have heard from women who attended the Freedom Programme.

Many women have described how much their lives and those of their children have improved without the Dominator. If YOU stop being the Dominator your partner will be able to live a peaceful safe life. She may even want to share it with you! How hard can it be?

Make a list of all the things women can actually do in a life which is free from abuse. Concentrate on small things, such as being able to eat food that they like.

Answers

....

....

....

....

....

Some examples which have been provided by women on the Freedom Programme.

We can make friends. We can invite friends home.
We can eat when we want.
We can wear what they want. We can work.
We can leave the children's toys out. The children can bring friends home.

Meal times are a pleasure. Children can sleep at night.
We can sleep at night.
We can choose when we want sex.
We can regain confidence again.
We can make contact with our families again.
We are free to come and go as we please.
We can choose our own underwear. Big knickers are often
mentioned as opposed to uncomfortable thongs.

Congratulations you have completed the course! **I do not include a
certificate because your improved behaviour is the only
acceptable evidence that you have done this work.**

Notes
Write your thoughts and feelings here to keep a record of your
progress through the programme.

....

....

....

....

....

....

....

....

....

....

....

Notes
Write your thoughts and feelings here to keep a record of your progress through the programme.

....

....

....

....

....

....

....

....

....

....

....

....

....

....

....

....

....

....

....

freedomprogramme@btinternet.com
www.freedomprogramme.co.uk

Printed in Great Britain
by Amazon